LONGMAN INTEGRATED SKILLS SERIES

Boost!
Reading 2

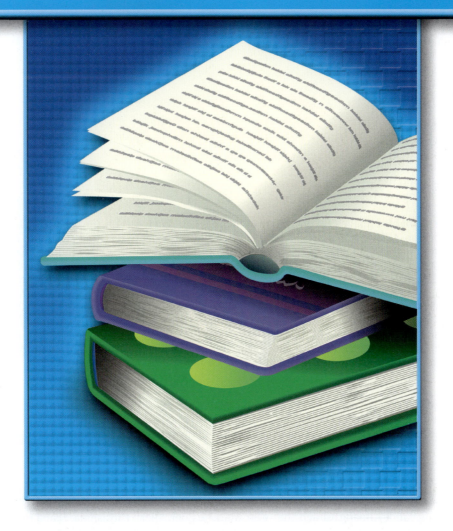

Jason Renshaw

Series Editors: Cecilia Petersen and Mayumi Tabuchi

PEARSON
Longman

Published by
Pearson Longman Asia ELT
20/F Cornwall House
Taikoo Place
979 King's Road
Quarry Bay
Hong Kong

fax: +852 2856 9578
email: pearsonlongman@pearsoned.com.hk
www.longman.com

and Associated Companies throughout the world.

© Pearson Education Asia Limited 2007

All rights reserved; no part of this publication may be reproduced, stored in a retrieval system, or transmitted in any form or by any means, electronic, mechanical, photocopying, recording, or otherwise without the prior written permission of the Publishers.

First published 2007
Reprinted 2007

Produced by Pearson Education Asia Limited, Hong Kong
GCC/02

ISBN-13: 978-962-00-5870-7
ISBN-10: 962-00-5870-4

Publisher: Simon Campbell
Project Editor: Howard Cheung
Editor: Michael Tom
Designers: Junko Funaki, Myth Wong
Illustrators: Balic Choy, Bernd Wong
Audio Production: David Pope and Sky Productions

For permission to use copyrighted images, we would like to thank © Gero Breloer/Epa/Corbis (pp. 4 CL and 9), © Munson, John/Star Ledger/Corbis (pp. 4 TR and 10 TR), © Rune Hellestad/Corbis (pp. 4 CC, 5 TL and TR, 10 BL, 12 TR and CL, 13 and 64), Getty Images (pp. 14, 49 BL and 53), AFP/Getty Images (pp. 5 BL and 17 CL), © Dewitt Jones/Corbis (pp. 5 BR and 17 BR), © Stephanie Maze/Corbis (p. 19), © Joseph Sohm; Visions of America/Corbis (p. 20 CR), © Susan Steinkamp/Corbis (p. 23), © Peter Beck/Corbis (p. 24), © Gary Braasch/Corbis (p. 27), © Jose Fuste Raga/Corbis (p. 29), © Catherine Karnow/Corbis (p. 30 TL), © Peter Adams/Corbis (p. 30 BL), © Bob Krist/Corbis (p. 30 TR), © Richard T. Nowitz/Corbis (p. 30 BR), © Atlantide Phototravel/Corbis (p. 32 CR), © Little Blue Wolf Productions/Corbis (p. 33), © Paul Hardy/Corbis (p. 34), © Dana Hoff/Beateworks/Corbis (p. 37 CR), © Charles Gullung/zefa/Corbis (p. 37 BR), Rob Reichenfeld © Dorling Kindersley (p. 47 CL and BR), © Images.com/Corbis (p. 49 T), © Judith Miller/Dorling Kindersley/Metropolis Collectibles, Inc. (pp. 50 CL and BR, and 52 TR), © Scott Stulberg/Corbis (p. 59), © Jim Craigmyle/Corbis (p. 60 BL) and © Petre Buzoianu/Corbis (p. 63).

Acknowledgements
These reading books are dedicated to my beloved wife, Yeona. Without her patience, support and encouragement, the Boost! series would not have been possible for me to write. Thank you also to the Korean teachers at Jasaeng JS English in Changwon, South Korea, who have been my partners in finding better ways to teach reading skills to young and teenage learners.
Jason Renshaw

The Publishers would also like to thank the following teachers for their suggestions and comments on this course:
Tara Cameron, Rosanne Cerello, Nancy Chan, Chang Li Ping, Joy Chao, Jessie Chen, Josephine Chen, Chiang Ying-hsueh, Claire Cho, Cindy Chuang, Linda Chuang, Chueh Shiu-wen, Mark de Boer, Mieko Hayashida, Diana Ho, Lulu Hsu, Eunice Jung, Hye Ri Kim, Jake Kimball, Josie Lai, Carol Lee, Elaine Lee, Melody Lee, Peggy Li, Esther Lim, Moon Jeong Lim, Jasmin Lin, Martin Lin, Catherine Littlehale Oki, Linda Liu, Tammy Liu, Goldie Luk, Ma Li-ling, Chizuko Matsushita, Geordie McGarty, Yasuyo Mito, Eunice Izumi Miyashita, Mari Nakamura, Yannick O'Neill, Coco Pan, Hannah Park, Karen Peng, Zanne Schultz, Kaj Schwermer, Mi Yeon Shin, Giant Shu, Dean Stafford, Hyunju Suh, Tan Yung-hui, Devon Thagard, John and Charlie van Goch, Annie Wang, Wang Shu-ling, Wu Lien-chun, Sabrina Wu, Yeh Shihfen, Tom Yeh, Laura Yoshida and Yunji Yun.

The publisher's policy is to use **paper manufactured from sustainable forests**

Welcome to

Boost! Reading 2

The **Boost!** Skills Series is the definitive and comprehensive four-level series of skills books for junior EFL learners. The series has been developed around age-appropriate, cross-curricular topics that develop students' critical thinking and examination techniques. It follows an integrated skills approach with each of the skills brought together at the end of each unit.

The twelve core units in **Boost! Reading 2** follow a clear and transparent structure to make teaching and learning easy and fun. The reading skills build and progress across the four levels of **Boost! Reading** and are correlated to the next generation of tests of English.

You will find the following in **Boost! Reading 2**:

- Age-appropriate and cross-curricular content-based passages
- A wide variety of text types (academic readings, reports, emails, newspaper articles, etc.)
- Units paired by theme, with a review unit for each pair

Unit Topic

Each unit has a cross-curricular and age-appropriate topic.

Students will
- find the topic directly relates to their own lives and study.
- be engaged and motivated to learn.

Reading

A graded, content-based reading passage, with supporting audio, sets up the main skill practice.

Students will
- find the reading passage stimulating with topics geared to their age level.
- be exposed to a variety of text types— from academic to real-world passages.
- be able to answer comprehension questions to aid understanding.

Reading Skill

A very simple introduction of the targeted unit skill is followed by a skill discovery activity.

Students will
- be introduced to the reading skill in a clear and understandable way.
- discover the reading skill for themselves without the need for long explanations.

Audio CD

The CD at the back of the book provides audio support for all reading passages plus the audio for the Integration listening tasks.

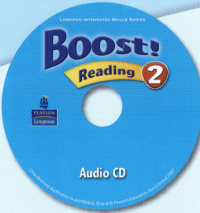

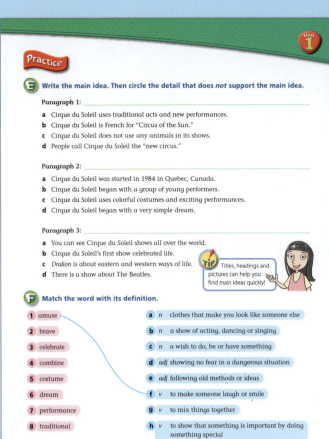

Practice

A skill practice task is followed by a vocabulary-building activity.

Students will
- be able to apply the reading skill to the passage through meaningful practice.
- develop their vocabulary by learning words in context.

Integration

The reading skill is combined with listening, writing or speaking tasks.

Students will
- learn to use a reading passage to springboard into productive activities.
- develop the language skills needed for the next generation of integrated tests of English.

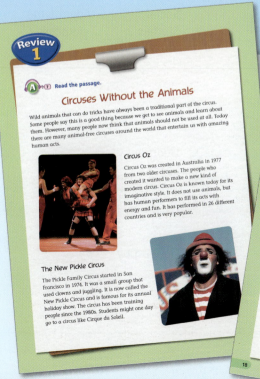

Review

After every two core units there is a review which consolidates the reading skills already studied.

Students will
- be able to see their progress in using reading skills.
- learn to apply different reading skills to the same passage.

Contents

Evaluation				p. 8

Unit	Subject	Reading skill	Text type	
Theme: Entertainment				
Unit 1 The New Circus	Culture and People	Finding main ideas and details	Content-based passage	p. 9
Unit 2 Amazing Talents	Sports and Leisure	Skimming and scanning	Interview	p. 13
Review 1				p. 17
Theme: The Environment				
Unit 3 Global Warming	Science/ Social Studies	Understanding difficult vocabulary	Content-based passage	p. 19
Unit 4 Save our planet!	Social Studies	Identifying purpose	Web log	p. 23
Review 2				p. 27
Theme: Travel and Places				
Unit 5 Great Cities	Geography/ Social Studies	Organizing information	Content-based passage	p. 29
Unit 6 Going Places	Geography	Understanding directions	Email	p. 33
Review 3				p. 37

Unit		Subject	Reading skill	Text type	
Theme: Ancient Greece					
Unit 7	At School	History	Making inferences	Content-based passage	p. 39
Unit 8	Fables	Myths/Social Studies	Understanding fables	Fables	p. 43
Review 4					p. 47
Theme: Superheroes					
Unit 9	Superheroes	Culture	Using previous knowledge	Content-based passage	p. 49
Unit 10	Movie Guides	Culture	Understanding guides	Movie guide	p. 53
Review 5					p. 57
Theme: The Internet					
Unit 11	Blogging	Technology	Understanding cause and effect	Content-based passage	p. 59
Unit 12	Online Forums	Culture and People	Understanding online forums	Online forum	p. 63
Review 6					p. 67
Mini-dictionary					p. 69

Evaluation

	Successful with the skill	Needs to review the skill	Comments
Unit 1 Finding main ideas and details			
Unit 2 Skimming and scanning			
Unit 3 Understanding difficult vocabulary			
Unit 4 Identifying purpose			
Unit 5 Organizing information			
Unit 6 Understanding directions			
Unit 7 Making inferences			
Unit 8 Understanding fables			
Unit 9 Using previous knowledge			
Unit 10 Understanding guides			
Unit 11 Understanding cause and effect			
Unit 12 Understanding online forums			

The New Circus

A What can you see at a circus? Discuss your answers.

Reading Skill

Finding main ideas and details

Main ideas are the most important ideas in a passage. Details give us different kinds of information to support the main ideas.

B Circle the main idea and underline two supporting details.

When you think of a circus, perhaps you think of big tents, funny clowns, acrobats, elephants and brave lion-tamers. Well, Cirque du Soleil (French for "Circus of the Sun") is a different kind of circus. Cirque du Soleil brings together traditional circus acts and new, creative performances. It does not use any animals.

The main idea is how Cirque du Soleil

a does not use animals.
b is French for "Circus of the Sun."
c is a different kind of circus.

Reading

2 Read the passage.

A Different Kind of Circus

When you think of a circus, perhaps you think of big tents, funny clowns, acrobats, elephants and brave lion-tamers. Well, Cirque du Soleil (French for "Circus of the Sun") is a different kind of circus. Cirque du Soleil combines traditional circus acts and new, creative performances. It does not use any animals. It uses ideas from street performances and different kinds of music and dance. People call Cirque du Soleil the "new circus."

Beginnings

Cirque du Soleil was started in 1984 in Quebec, Canada, by two street performers. It began with a very simple dream. A group of young performers got together to amuse people, see the world and have fun doing it. The circus quickly became famous for its creativity, colorful costumes and exciting performances.

Touring Shows

Cirque du Soleil has created many shows that travel all over the world. Their first show, *Saltimbanco*, celebrated life. *Alegría* is about hope. *Quidam* is set in the imaginary world of a sad and lonely girl. *Dralion* is about eastern and western ways of life. There is even a show that tells the story of The Beatles, called *LOVE*.

D Answer the questions.

1. What does "Cirque du Soleil" mean?
2. When was Cirque du Soleil started?
3. What is *Alegría* about?

Practice

 E Write the main idea. Then circle the detail that does *not* support the main idea.

Paragraph 1: _____

a   Cirque du Soleil uses traditional acts and new performances.
b   Cirque du Soleil is French for "Circus of the Sun."
c   Cirque du Soleil does not use any animals in its shows.
d   People call Cirque du Soleil the "new circus."

Paragraph 2: _____

a   Cirque du Soleil was started in 1984 in Quebec, Canada.
b   Cirque du Soleil began with a group of young performers.
c   Cirque du Soleil uses colorful costumes and exciting performances.
d   Cirque du Soleil began with a very simple dream.

Paragraph 3: _____

a   You can see Cirque du Soleil shows all over the world.
b   Cirque du Soleil's first show celebrated life.
c   *Dralion* is about eastern and western ways of life.
d   There is a show about The Beatles.

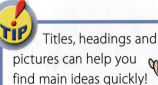 **TIP** Titles, headings and pictures can help you find main ideas quickly!

F Match the word with its definition.

1 amuse
2 brave
3 celebrate
4 combine
5 costume
6 dream
7 performance
8 traditional

a   *n*   clothes that make you look like someone else
b   *n*   a show of acting, dancing or singing
c   *n*   a wish to do, be or have something
d   *adj* showing no fear in a dangerous situation
e   *adj* following old methods or ideas
f   *v*   to make someone laugh or smile
g   *v*   to mix things together
h   *v*   to show that something is important by doing something special

11

Integration

G 3 **Read about *Dralion*.**

Dralion by Cirque du Soleil is an interesting combination of eastern and western circus acts. It combines traditional Asian acts with its own modern creativity and color. Even the name "Dralion" shows this mix of East and West. People from both eastern and western countries enjoy *Dralion*!

H 4 **Listen and complete the paragraph.**

Dralion's mix of (1) __performances__ from the East and West is great to see. There are (2)_____ like "bamboo poles" and "hoop diving," as well as clowns and juggling. The name of the (3)_____ is actually a combination of "dragon" from the East and "(4)_____" from the West. *Dralion* is very (5)_____ all over Asia, North (6)_____ and Europe.

I Work with a classmate. Combine details that are similar from Activities G and H above.

> *Dralion* by Cirque du Soleil is an interesting combination of eastern and western circus acts.

> Yes, its mix of performances from the East and West is great to see.

Amazing Talents

Unit 2

A What is your favorite circus act? Discuss your answers.

Reading Skill

Skimming and scanning

When you skim, you read quickly without reading every word. It can help you find the main ideas. When you scan, you look carefully to try to find key words that can show you where important details are.

B Skim the article on page 14 and write the main idea. Then scan the article for the key words. Time yourself to see how fast you are.

Main idea: _____ (_____ mins. _____ secs.)

Key words: *Dralion*   (_____ mins. _____ secs.)   fun   (_____ mins. _____ secs.)

mom   (_____ mins. _____ secs.)   games   (_____ mins. _____ secs.)

Reading

5 Read the article.

Life as a Balancing Act

Meet Zhao Yasi from China. At 16, she is one of the youngest performers for Cirque du Soleil. Yasi stars as a hand balancer in the fantastic *Dralion* show. Our reporter Alex Brown interviewed Yasi to find out about her life as a circus performer.

Alex: Hi, Yasi! How did you become a hand balancer?

Yasi: When I was very young I was always running around. So my mom thought I might like being in a circus. She was right! After a while I just concentrated on hand balancing.

Alex: You make it look easy but I'm sure it's not! How long does it take to learn?

Yasi: A long time! It took five years for me to learn how to balance well. It's really hard work. During my act, I balance on one hand for more than seven minutes while doing my movements.

Alex: Sounds tough! Is life in the circus fun?

Yasi: Yes, of course! It's great going to so many different countries and cities. There are other performers in the show who are my good friends. After a show we watch DVDs and play games.

Alex: Is there a downside?

Yasi: Yes, I don't get to see my family very often and sometimes I'm homesick.

D Answer the questions.

1. In what show does Yasi star?
2. How does Yasi feel about going to different countries and cities with the circus?
3. What do Yasi and her friends do after a show?

Practice

E Write the best key words to scan for. Then scan the article and write the answers.

1. What is the name of the reporter?   Scan for: _reporter_
   Alex Brown.

2. What was Yasi like when she was very young?   Scan for: _____

3. How long did it take Yasi to learn to hand balance well?   Scan for: _____

4. In her act, how long does Yasi balance on one hand?   Scan for: _____

5. Who are Yasi's good friends?   Scan for: _____

6. Who does Yasi want to see more often?   Scan for: _____

TIP Look for key words in the questions.

F Match the word with its definition.

1. balance
2. concentrate
3. downside
4. homesick
5. interview
6. movement
7. reporter
8. tough

a. n   when something moves from one place to another
b. n   the negative or bad part of something
c. n   someone who writes for a newspaper
d. adj   difficult to do
e. adj   feeling unhappy because you are far from home
f. v   to be in a position where you will not fall over
g. v   to use most of your attention and time to do one thing
h. v   to ask someone questions for a newspaper

 6 Read the interview with Ben.

Anna: How did you start juggling, Ben?

Ben: When I was six, my dad bought me some juggling balls for my birthday and showed me some basics skills. I loved it from the start.

Anna: Do you practice a lot?

Ben: Yes, every day. I usually do an hour in the morning before school. After school, I practice for about two hours once I've finished my homework.

Anna: Do you have time for other activities?

Ben: Well, I try to do other things, too, like swimming and playing games online.

Anna: So do you want to join a circus in the future?

Ben: Yes! I love juggling and it must be fun being in a circus.

 Choose a classmate to interview about his or her special skill. First, prepare three questions to ask. Then interview your classmate and make notes for each answer.

Classmate: _____

Interview about: _____

	Question	Notes for answer
1		
2		
3		

 Tell the class about your classmate's special skill.

 Read the passage.

Circuses Without the Animals

Wild animals that can do tricks have always been a traditional part of the circus. Some people say this is a good thing because we get to see animals and learn about them. However, many people now think that animals should not be used at all. Today there are many animal-free circuses around the world that entertain us with amazing human acts.

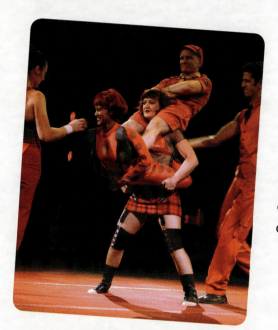

Circus Oz

Circus Oz was created in Australia in 1977 from two older circuses. The people who created it wanted to make a new kind of modern circus. Circus Oz is known today for its imaginative style. It does not use animals, but has human performers to fill its acts with energy and fun. It has performed in 26 different countries and is very popular.

The New Pickle Circus

The Pickle Family Circus started in San Francisco in 1974. It was a small group that used clowns and juggling. It is now called the New Pickle Circus and is famous for its annual holiday show. The circus has been training people since the 1980s. Students might one day go to a circus like Cirque du Soleil.

B **Circle the correct answer.**

1. The main idea of paragraph 1 is
   a. it is traditional to use wild animals in circuses.
   b. some people want animals in circuses but others do not like the idea.
   c. animal-free circuses are more entertaining.
   d. animal-free circuses are more entertaining than traditional circuses.

2. The main idea of paragraph 2 is
   a. Circus Oz is very popular.
   b. Circus Oz is one of the oldest circuses in Australia.
   c. Circus Oz is a new and modern circus.
   d. Circus Oz travels to many different countries.

3. The main idea of paragraph 3 is
   a. the holiday show at the New Pickle Circus.
   b. the history of the New Pickle Circus.
   c. the connection between the New Pickle Circus and Cirque du Soleil.
   d. the training at the New Pickle Circus.

4. Some people think having animals in circuses is a good thing because
   a. we get to see them and learn about them.
   b. they are a traditional part of the circus.
   c. they can do tricks.
   d. they can entertain us with amazing acts.

5. Circus Oz is known for
   a. its human performers.
   b. being popular with audiences.
   c. being created in Australia.
   d. its imaginative style.

6. The New Pickle Circus is famous for
   a. clowns and juggling.
   b. its holiday show.
   c. training people.
   d. its students.

Global Warming

Unit 3

A What do you know about global warming? Discuss your answers.

Reading Skill

Understanding difficult vocabulary

You can often find out the meaning of difficult new words or phrases, such as scientific names, by looking for explanations the writer might have included.

B Underline the part that tells you what the circled word means.

When sunlight reaches the earth, the (atmosphere) (which is the mix of gases around the earth) stops some of the heat from going back out into space. This is called the greenhouse effect. It is important for (maintaining)—carrying on—life on earth.

Reading

C 8 **Read the passage.**

Global Warming

Warming up ...

Scientists are saying that the earth is getting warmer. The earth's temperature—how hot or cold it is—has been rising, and the problem is getting worse. This is known as global warming.

The Greenhouse Effect

When sunlight reaches the earth, the atmosphere (which is the mix of gases around the earth) stops some of the heat from going back out into space. This is called the greenhouse effect. It is important for maintaining—carrying on—life on earth.

What are greenhouse gases?

Greenhouse gases are the gases in the atmosphere that actually trap the heat we get from sunlight. Carbon dioxide is one of the most important greenhouse gases.

So what is the problem?

Human activity (the things people do) is making levels of greenhouse gases in the atmosphere rise. Burning fossil fuels (like coal and oil) and cutting down trees are examples of this. It is making the earth warmer than it should be.

What could happen?

In the next hundred years, the earth could become a lot warmer. The ice at the poles, or the most northern and southern points of the earth, could melt. This will make the sea level rise and many cities could be flooded. Many kinds of animals and plants could become extinct— meaning they die out forever.

D **Answer the questions.**

1. Why is the greenhouse effect important?
2. Which human activities cause levels of greenhouse gases to rise?
3. What could happen if the sea level rises?

Practice

E Write what the word or phrase from the passage means.

1 temperature

_____

_____

2 atmosphere

_____

_____

3 maintaining

_____

_____

4 poles

_____

_____

5 become extinct

_____

_____

TIP Look closely for explanations just after the word or phrase in the passage.

F Match the word with its definition.

1 burn
2 level
3 flood
4 global
5 heat
6 melt
7 space
8 trap

a *n* high temperature
b *n* the place beyond the earth
c *n* the amount of something compared to another amount
d *adj* about the whole world
e *v* to destroy something with fire
f *v* to keep something from getting out
g *v* to become covered in water
h *v* to change into liquid form

21

 Read about how global warming worries Amy and Ben.

I worry most about the weather being too hot. Maybe we can never go outside!

I worry most about different kinds of animals becoming extinct. Maybe there won't be any interesting animals left.

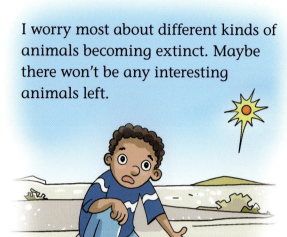

 What worries you most about global warming? Write what you and four classmates think.

Name	Worry most about	Reason
1 Me		
2		
3		
4		
5		

 Tell the class.

> Robbie worries most about the sea level rising. He thinks maybe his home will be flooded.

22

Save our planet!

Unit 4

A What can you do to help stop global warming? Discuss your answers.

Reading Skill

Identifying purpose

The purpose of a passage is what the writer wanted it to do. Knowing the purpose will help you better understand the writing.

B Look at the passages on pages 10, 14 and 20. Match them to the correct purpose.

1 A Different Kind of Circus (Unit 1)
2 Life as a Balancing Act (Unit 2)
3 Global Warming (Unit 3)

a To tell us about a Cirque du Soleil performer named Zhao Yasi.
b To tell us how gobal warming happens.
c To tell us about Cirque du Soleil's history and shows.

23

Reading

C 🎧 10 **Read the blog entry.**

Billy's SOP blog

Jan. Feb. Mar. **Apr.** May June July Aug. Sept. Oct. Nov. Dec.

This month's **goals** for helping to **SAVE OUR PLANET!**

1. Save **electricity**
2. **Recycle**
3. Save water
4. Save gas

"My sister, Jessica, recycling."

Week 1 – This week, my family tried to use less electricity. We turned off lights when no one was in the room. We switched off the TV when nobody was watching it. Mom used cold water instead of hot water in the washing machine.

Week 2 – We started recycling this week. We divided our **trash** into different bags for bottles, cans, paper and food. Mom kept the **plastic** shopping bags from the supermarket to use again as trash bags. These are great ways to help our **environment**!

Week 3 – We stopped taking baths and had short showers instead. Mom and Dad used less water in the kettle when they made tea or coffee. My sister and I didn't leave the tap running when we brushed our teeth.

Week 4 – My sister and I started riding our bikes to school instead of having Mom drive us. It's hard work, but good exercise! Dad and a few of the people he works with also started to **carpool** this week. This should help **reduce** greenhouse gases!

D **Answer the questions.**

1. What does "SOP" stand for?
2. What did Billy's mom do with the shopping bags?
3. How did Billy and his sister save water in Week 3?

Practice

 E Circle the correct purpose.

Week 1

a To show how we can use less electricity.
b To explain why we should use less electricity.
c To explain the importance of electricity.
d To tell us why we waste electricity.

Week 4

a To show how we can use less gas.
b To explain how saving gas reduces greenhouse gases.
c To describe how hard it is to save gas.
d To tell us that carpooling works.

The whole blog entry
(circle two answers)

a To tell us why we should help "save our planet."
b To show how a family can help "save our planet."
c To explain why the environment and greenhouse gases are important.
d To give examples of how we can help "save our planet."

TIP Find the purpose for each section. Then combine them to identify the main purposes.

 F Match the word with its definition.

1	carpool	a	n	something you hope to complete successfully in the future
2	electricity	b	n	things you throw away
3	environment	c	n	the power that is used to make machines work or to provide light or heat
4	goal	d	n	the air, water and land on earth
5	plastic	e	adj	made from a light strong material
6	recycle	f	v	to make less or smaller in size
7	reduce	g	v	to travel together in one car and share the cost
8	trash	h	v	to treat something that has been used so it can be used again

25

G 🎧 11 Read the notes for an SOP plan.

Goal	Idea
1 Save electricity!	• Turn off my computer when I am not using it.
2 Save paper!	• Write on both sides of paper instead of just on one side. • Keep envelopes I get in the mail and use them again for my own letters.
3 Save water!	• Take shorter showers. • Catch rainwater and use it for watering the plants on days when there is no rain.
4 Plant trees!	• Ask Mom to plant trees instead of flowers in the yard.

H Write notes for your own SOP plan.

Goal	Idea
1	
2	
3	
4	

I Write an SOP blog on a separate piece of paper. Show how you will achieve your SOP goals.

 Read the notice.

Let's be more earth friendly!

Dear Students,

Please help make our school more earth friendly. We want to minimize—reduce as much as possible—the amount of water we use. We also want to recycle paper, cans and bottles. So please try to follow these new school rules:

1) Try to use less water when you are washing your hands.
2) Try to write on both sides of your paper, not just on one side.
3) Place paper, cans and bottles in the specially labeled recycling bins.

We also hope you will volunteer—which is working without pay—as one of our Earth Friends. These are the programs you can join:

A) The Plant It program:
Students plant more trees around the school grounds.

B) The Bike It program:
Students ride their bicycles to school every day.

C) The Pool It program:
Families that live near each other carpool.

Good luck and thank you for helping our school become more earth friendly!

Mrs. Anderson
School Principal

Review 2

B **Circle the correct answer.**

1. The main idea of the notice is
   a. the new school rules.
   b. ways to make the school earth friendly.
   c. the different Earth Friends volunteer programs.
   d. the importance of recycling.

2. The school wants to minimize the amount of
   a. paper, cans and bottles they use.
   b. money they spend on Earth Friends programs.
   c. water they use.
   d. paper that is recycled.

3. Students with bicycles can join the
   a. Plant It program.
   b. Earth Friends.
   c. Pool It program.
   d. Bike It program.

4. The main purpose of the notice is
   a. to explain new school rules and ask students to become Earth Friends.
   b. to wish students luck and thank them.
   c. to show that the school has Earth Friends who are volunteers.
   d. to describe how the school is earth friendly.

C **Write what the word means.**

1. minimize _____
2. volunteer _____

Great Cities

A Why do people live in cities? Discuss your answers.

Reading Skill

Organizing information

When there are many similar kinds of details, it is useful to organize them. A good way to do this is to put them into a table.

B Complete the table headings and details.

Mumbai is a city on the west coast of India. It is one of the biggest cities in the world, with a population of over 18 million people. London is the capital of the United Kingdom. It is in the south of the country and has a population of around eight million people.

		Region	Population
Mumbai	India		
London		south	

Reading

 Read the passage.

Great Cities of the World

What makes a city a great city? Here is some information about four of the world's most famous cities.

Mumbai

Mumbai is a city on the west coast of India. It is one of the biggest cities in the world, with a population of over 18 million people. Mumbai is famous for its national park and being the home of "Bollywood," where most Indian movies are made.

London

London is the capital of the United Kingdom. It is in the south of the country and has a population of around eight million people. London was created by the Romans in A.D. 43. It is well known for its many landmarks, such as Big Ben and the London Eye.

Shanghai

Shanghai is the largest city in China, with a population of over 14 million people. It was founded in 1553 and is on the east coast. Shanghai is known for its spectacular skyline, the famous Nanjing Road shopping area and its busy port.

Rio de Janeiro

Rio de Janeiro, with a population of around 11 million people, is one of the biggest cities in Brazil. It was founded in 1565 and is famous for its carnival (street party), beaches and a large statue on a mountain looking over the city.

D Answer the questions.

1 Where is "Bollywood"?
2 When was London founded?
3 What looks over Rio de Janeiro?

Practice

E Complete the table headings and organize the information from the passage.

City		London		
Country				
Region				—
Population	18 million			
	—		1553	
				carnival, beaches, statue on a mountain

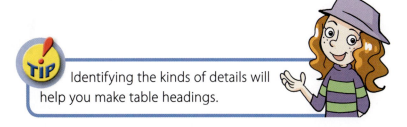

Identifying the kinds of details will help you make table headings.

F Write the word for each definition.

> capital   coast   found   landmark   population   port   skyline   spectacular

1. **landmark**
   n something that helps you recognize where you are

2. _____
   n land next to the sea

3. _____
   n an area or town where ships arrive and leave

4. _____
   n the outline of buildings against the sky

5. _____
   n a city where the main government of a country is

6. _____
   n number of people living in an area

7. _____
   adj very impressive and dramatic

8. _____
   v to start something such as a city or company

31

Integration

G 🎧14 Listen and complete the paragraph.

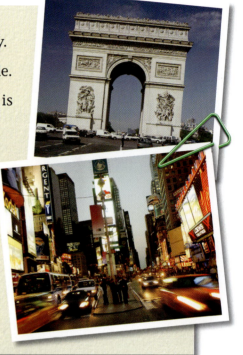

Paris is the **(1)**_____ of France and its largest city. It has a population of more than **(2)**_____ people. Paris was founded by the Romans in **(3)**_____ It is famous for its **(4)**_____, beautiful buildings, fashion, arts and culture.

New York City was **(5)**_____ in 1613 by the Dutch. It is the **(6)**_____ city in the United States with a **(7)**_____ of around eight million people. It is famous for its **(8)**_____, entertainment and arts.

H Complete the table headings and organize the information about the two cities.

City	Paris	New York City

I Work with a classmate. Compare the two cities.

- Paris is the largest city in France.
- New York City is the largest city in the United States.

Going Places

Unit 6

A What places would you like to visit? Discuss your answers.

Reading Skill

Understanding directions
Directions are instructions that tell how you to get somewhere. They usually refer to names of places or things to look out for.

B Follow the directions. Mark an "X" where the house is.

From the train station, you should walk along Green Street. When you reach Grandview Street, cross over to the bakery. Continue down Green Street until you get to the shoe store. Cross over to the pharmacy, and then over Treeview Road. Turn right and walk a little way till you get to Bluejay Street. Turn left and walk along the street. The house is on your left.

33

 Read the email.

From: salkendry@kidstarmail.co.uk
To: jrp@freemail4all.com
Sent: Sat., Aug. 3
Subject: Directions for the London Underground (the Tube)

Hey, Jina!

I'm so glad you're coming to stay! Let me give you some directions from the airport. You can also download a Tube map from the London Underground's website (www.tfl.gov.uk). Anyway, I hope you understand my instructions!

From Heathrow, get on the Tube—there's only the Piccadilly Line there. You'll pass a lot of stations, but you need to get off and change at Piccadilly Circus. From there, you should take the Bakerloo Line to Oxford Circus. It's only one stop, so don't miss it! At Oxford Circus, you have to change again. You need the red Central Line. It's a bit complicated so make sure you get the right platform. Head to Marble Arch. It's just two stops away—the one after Bond Street. My house is really close to Marble Arch Station—it's really convenient. Just give me a call when you arrive and I'll come and get you!

It's not the shortest route here, but I think it's the simplest. If you have any problems, just ask the other passengers. The Tube staff will always help you, too.

Looking forward to seeing you soon!

Love,
Sally

 Answer the questions.

1   What is the name of the airport?

2   How many Tube lines are there from the airport?

3   Who can help Jina if she has problems?

Practice

E Circle the correct answer.

1. Which station should Jina change at first?
   a. Oxford Circus
   b. Piccadilly Circus
   c. Marble Arch
   d. Bond Street

2. What does Jina have to do at Oxford Circus?
   a. Change to the Piccadilly Line.
   b. Change to the Bakerloo Line.
   c. Change to the Central Line.
   d. Stay on the same line.

3. Which line is Marble Arch on?
   a. Bakerloo Line
   b. Piccadilly Line
   c. Central Line
   d. Oxford Line

4. Where is Bond Street on the Central Line?
   a. Between Oxford Circus and Marble Arch.
   b. One stop after Piccadilly Circus.
   c. Between Piccadilly Circus and Oxford Circus.
   d. Close to Sally's house.

TIP The best way to understand directions is to break them up into simple steps.

F Write the word for each definition.

| complicated   convenient   head   miss   passenger   platform   route   stop |

1. *n* someone who is traveling in a vehicle, but not driving
2. *n* the raised place where you get on and off a train
3. *n* the way from one place to another
4. *n* a place where a train or bus picks up or drops off people
5. *adj* near and easy to get to
6. *adj* difficult to understand because it has many details
7. *v* to not notice a train or bus stop until it has passed
8. *v* to go towards a particular place

G 🎧 16 Look at the map and complete the email.

From: scott.hanson@gomail.net
To: steve123@freemail4all.com
Sent: Thurs., Nov. 23
Subject: Directions!

Hi, Stevie!

Here are some directions for when you arrive at the train station. Good luck!

1. Take bus 73X. It should cost about $4.50.
2. Get off when you see the **(1)**_____ called Bookmarks.
3. Walk up Main Drive, past the big **(2)**_____.
4. At the **(3)**_____, turn right onto **(4)**_____.
5. **(5)**_____ Towers is on the **(6)**_____—you can't miss it.

Looking forward to seeing you!
Scott

H Write directions from your school to your home.

Direction 1: _____

Direction 2: _____

Direction 3: _____

Direction 4: _____

Direction 5: _____

I Tell the class how to get to your home.

Review 3

A **Read the emails.**

| To: | tommymc@emailstar.net | Sent: | Fri., June 16 |
| From: | pmorecroft@homestay.com.ca | Subject: | Homestay options |

Dear Tommy,

I am happy to tell you that we have four lovely Canadian host families for you to choose from.

The first family is the Richardsons. They have a big house with four bedrooms on Smith Street, two children (a boy aged 12 and a girl aged 16) and a dog. The O'Neills have a medium-sized house with three bedrooms on Orion Road, a son aged 11 and some pet birds. The Staffords have a small three-bedroom house on Steep Street, a daughter aged 7 and no pets. The Wilsons are in a very large house (five bedrooms) on Orion Road. They have a boy aged 12 and a girl aged 7. They also have a little turtle.

Please let us know which family you would like to stay with for your homestay.

Sincerely,
Patrick Morecroft
Homestay Coordinator

| To: | tommymc@emailstar.net | Date: | Sun., July 30 |
| From: | maryrichardson@kidstarmail.com | Subject: | Directions |

Hi Tommy!

It's very easy to get here from the bus station. Just go up Orion Road and turn right at the store onto Berry Street. Cross over the bridge and go past the big supermarket. Turn right at the gas station onto Smith Street. We're at number 24—it's on the right-hand side.

See you soon!
Mary

37

B Circle the correct answer.

1 The main purpose of Patrick's email is
   a to recommend a family for Tommy to stay with.
   b to describe the children in each family.
   c to explain the rules of the homestay.
   d to ask Tommy which family he would like to stay with.

2 The main purpose of Mary's email is
   a to tell Tommy how to get to the house.
   b to tell Tommy that the house is easy to get to.
   c to tell Tommy about her family.
   d to tell Tommy where the supermarket is.

C Organize the information about the different families.

	Richardson	O'Neill	Stafford	Wilson
Location				
House size				
Bedrooms				
Children				
Pets				

D Draw the route Mary describes and mark an "X" where the house is.

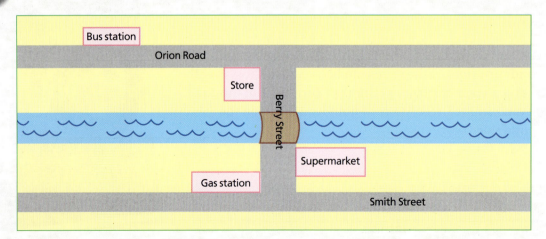

At School — Unit 7

A What are your favorite subjects at school? Discuss your answers.

Reading Skill

Making inferences

You can make inferences (smart guesses) about what you read by thinking about what it could mean or how you could say it in a different way.

B Match the inference with the underlined detail it comes from.

Boys in ancient Greece had hobbies like **A** fishing and sailing. **B** At age six or seven, most of them started to go to school. In most places, girls did not go to school. They **C** stayed at home and learned from their mothers.

1 Boys knew how to use boats. ☐
2 Girls learned how to do housework. ☐
3 Most eight-year-old boys were in school. ☐

Reading

C 18 Read the passage.

Education in Ancient Greece

The ancient Greeks were great builders and thinkers. Their ideas still influence us today, especially in the arts, science, literature and philosophy. But school for boys and girls in ancient Greece was very different than today.

School for Boys

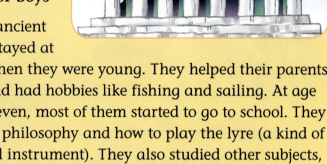

Boys in ancient Greece stayed at home when they were young. They helped their parents work and had hobbies like fishing and sailing. At age six or seven, most of them started to go to school. They studied philosophy and how to play the lyre (a kind of musical instrument). They also studied other subjects, but they did not use many books. Most of what they learned was said out loud and memorized.

School for Girls

In most places in ancient Greece, girls did not go to school. They stayed at home and learned from their mothers. Girls were not allowed to go outside the house much. However, things were different for girls in a part of Greece called Sparta. Girls there went to military school where they learned how to wrestle and fight! This was to prepare them for joining the army. Girls in Sparta were allowed to go outside the house a lot more.

D Answer the questions.

1. In which subjects do ancient Greek ideas still influence us?
2. What instrument did boys learn to play?
3. In which part of ancient Greece were girls allowed to go to school?

Practice

 Circle the correct answer.

1. From paragraph 1, we can infer that the ancient Greeks
   a. studied many subjects.
   b. had very good ideas.
   c. built great schools.
   d. were hard-working.

2. From paragraph 2, we can infer that the ancient Greeks
   a. did not like books.
   b. were talented musicians.
   c. made the best sailboats.
   d. thought education was important.

3. From paragraph 3, we can infer that in ancient Sparta,
   a. boys and girls were treated more equally than in other parts of Greece.
   b. girls never helped their mothers do housework.
   c. boys and girls went to the same schools.
   d. girls were better fighters than the boys.

TIP Check the details in each paragraph and think carefully about what they can mean.

 Write the word for each definition.

| ancient | army | influence | literature | memorize | military | philosophy | wrestle |

1. n books, poems and plays that are important

2. n the study of ideas about thought and actions

3. n a large group of soldiers who are trained to fight on land

4. adj about a country's army or navy

5. adj happening or existing a long time ago

6. v to learn something completely so that you remember it exactly

7. v to fight by holding or pushing

8. v to affect the way someone thinks or acts

41

Integration

G 🎧 19 Read about Mike's and Kate's favorite school subjects and clubs.

My favorite subjects are science, English and P.E. I'm in the Young Inventors Club.

My favorite subjects are math, science and computing. I'm in the Rock Climbing Club.

H What are your favorite school subjects and clubs? Write what you and four classmates think.

Name	Favorite subjects	Club
1 Me		
2		
3		
4		
5		

I Tell the class.

Jill's favorite subjects are English and history. She's in the Chess Club.

Fables — Unit 8

A What are these stories about? Discuss your answers.

The Boy Who Cried Wolf

The Ant and the Grasshopper

Reading Skill

Understanding fables

A fable is a short story that teaches you a lesson in how to think or behave. The characters in fables are usually animals.

B Read the beginning of a fable and circle what you think the fable will be about.

In the summer, an ant was busy preparing for the winter. He was collecting as much food as he could. A grasshopper saw the ant and laughed, "Why are you working, ant? It's summer and I'm singing and having fun."

a food
b being lazy
c the seasons

Reading

C 20 **Read the fables.**

Aesop's Fables

Thousands of years ago, a Greek writer named Aesop wrote a set of fables. They were short and simple, and were designed to teach us important lessons. Aesop's fables are still used today. Here are two of his most famous fables.

The Boy Who Cried Wolf
A shepherd boy found a new way to have fun. He cried, "Wolf! Wolf! A wolf is eating the sheep!" The people from his village came running to help him, but only to find that it was a lie. The boy played this trick a few more times and the villagers did not trust him anymore. One day, a wolf did come and started eating the sheep. The boy quickly cried, "Wolf! A real wolf!" However, no one came to help him because they did not believe him. All his sheep were eaten.

The Ant and the Grasshopper
In the summer, an ant was busy preparing for the winter. He was collecting as much food as he could. A grasshopper saw the ant and laughed, "Why are you working, ant? It's summer and I'm singing and having fun." Later, when winter came, the idle grasshopper went hungry because he had nothing to eat. But the hard-working ant was now happy because he had a lot of food for the winter.

D **Answer the questions.**

1. Where did Aesop come from?
2. When the wolf came, why did no one help the boy?
3. Why was the ant collecting food?

Practice

E Circle the best answer.

1 The lesson of *The Boy Who Cried Wolf* is
   a telling the truth is better than telling lies.
   b do not play tricks on people too often.
   c do not help people because they might be telling lies.
   d do not tell lies because people will not believe you when you tell the truth.

2 The lesson of *The Ant and the Grasshopper* is
   a it is a good idea to work hard now and be prepared for later.
   b you should always try to work hard and not have too much fun.
   c you should enjoy yourself now because you might not be able to later.
   d do not worry about what others say to you.

TIP Fables usually teach you how to live or think in an honest and positive way.

F Write the word for each definition.

| collect   hard-working   idle   lie   prepare   shepherd   trick   trust |

1 n something you do to make someone believe something that is not true

2 n someone who takes care of sheep

3 n something you say that you know is untrue

4 adj lazy or not working

5 adj working with a lot of effort

6 v to get things and bring them together

7 v to believe that someone will not do anything bad

8 v to make plans for something

Integration

G 🎧 21 **Read the new version of** *The Boy Who Cried Wolf.*

A boy found a new way to have fun. He cried, "Help! Help! A thief is robbing my house!" The people from the other houses came running to help him, but only to find that it was a lie. The boy played this trick a few more times and the people did not trust him anymore. One day, a thief did come and started robbing the house. The boy quickly cried, "Help! A real thief!" However, no one came to help him because they did not believe him. The boy lost many things from his house.

H **Plan your own version of** *The Ant and the Grasshopper.*

	The Ant and the Grasshopper	Your version
Times	summer, then winter	
Characters	an ant and a grasshopper	
Actions	ant: collecting food grasshopper: singing, having fun	
Results	ant: food for winter grasshopper: no food for winter	

I **Tell the class your version of** *The Ant and the Grasshopper.*

Review 4

A **Read the passage.**

The Parthenon

The Parthenon is a temple that was built in the fifth century B.C. in Athens, Greece. The ancient Greeks built the temple in honor of the goddess Athena. The city's name also comes from the goddess's name. The Parthenon is one of the oldest and finest examples of the ancient Greeks' great building skills.

There are many amazing features of the Parthenon. One example is the columns of the temple. The builders of the Parthenon made the columns curve out, so they were a little wider in the middle. This trick makes the columns look straight when viewed from below.

Even though it has been badly damaged and many things have been stolen from it, the Parthenon is still spectacular. It can be seen from most parts of Athens. Every year, many thousands of tourists visit the Parthenon. Because it is more than 2,500 years old, it is one of the most important buildings in the world.

B **Circle the correct answer.**

1. The main idea of paragraph 2 is
   a. the Parthenon's columns curve out.
   b. there are many amazing features of the Parthenon, like its columns.
   c. columns are used on the sides of the temple.
   d. the Parthenon's columns look straight from below.

2. Athens was named after
   a. a temple.
   b. a goddess.
   c. the Parthenon.
   d. another city.

3. The main purpose of the passage is
   a. to describe the importance of Greek buildings.
   b. to show that the Parthenon is a popular and beautiful place.
   c. to explain why the anciet Greeks were great builders.
   d. to explain the Parthenon's history and why it is popular.

4. From paragraph 1, we can infer that
   a. Greek cities took their names from temples.
   b. the ancient Greeks built many temples.
   c. Athena was important to the ancient Greeks.
   d. the Parthenon was expensive to build.

5. From paragraph 2, we can infer that
   a. the ancient Greeks were very skillful builders.
   b. the Parthenon's curved columns made the temple stronger.
   c. the Parthenon can only be viewed from below.
   d. the Parthenon has three amazing features that trick our eyes.

6. From paragraph 3, we can infer that the Parthenon
   a. was damaged during Greek wars.
   b. gets a lot of tourists because it is so old.
   c. is the tallest building in Athens.
   d. was not protected well in the past.

Superheroes — Unit 9

A Who is your favorite superhero? Discuss your answers.

Reading Skill

Using previous knowledge

Your previous knowledge is what you already know about something before you read about it. It can help you better understand what you are reading.

B Do you know the name of this superhero? Write what you know about him.

Name: _____

Previous knowledge: _____

_____

_____

 Read the passage.

Comic Book Heroes

Comic books are a special kind of storybook. They tell a story using only pictures and speech bubbles or captions. The characters at the heart—or center—of these stories are usually superheroes with special abilities.

Spider-Man

The Spider-Man comic books follow the adventures of a young man named A Peter Parker. Peter's parents died when he was young so he lives with his aunt and uncle. Peter gained his spider-like abilities B when he was 15. He made many clever gadgets himself C , such as his web-shooters. He uses his skills to fight evil enemies, like the Green Goblin and D Venom. Peter is E very different when he is Spider-Man—he becomes strong and brave.

Storm

Storm F is the name of a female superhero G from the X-Men comic books. The X-Men are mutants born with superhero abilities. They H team together to fight other mutants, like the evil Magneto, Sabretooth and Toad. Storm can I fly and J fight using her special ability to control the weather.

 Answer the questions.

1 What makes comic books special?

2 How does Peter's character change when he is Spider-Man?

3 What are Storm's abilities?

E Find the part of the passage that each new detail refers to.

Spider-Man
1 Venom and Spider-Man have similar abilities. **D**
2 Peter's full name is Peter Benjamin Parker.
3 Peter is a shy, quiet person normally.
4 Peter is interested in science and inventing things.
5 Peter gained his abilities after getting bitten by a special spider.

TIP See if the detail explains something or gives you extra information about things mentioned in the passage.

Storm
6 The X-Men were founded by a mutant named Professor X.
7 Storm's real name is Ororo Munroe.
8 Storm can make the air carry her around.
9 Female superheroes are sometimes called superheroines.
10 Storm can use strong winds or lightning to hit her enemies.

F Find and write the word next to its definition.

1 _mutant_   n   an animal or person whose body is different from others of the same kind

2 _____   n   a character in storybooks who uses special powers to help others

3 _____   n   an exciting experience

4 _____   n   a skill or power to do something

5 _____   n   a cleverly designed machine or tool

6 _____   n   an explanation for a picture

7 _____   n   someone who wants to harm you

8 _____   v   to make someone or something do what you want

51

Integration

G 🎧 24 **Read about Batman.**

Batman is one of the world's first superheroes. He has many skills and is very clever. He wears a special costume to make him look like a bat. He also has many clever gadgets to help him fight his enemies. Batman has a friend who helps him, named Robin. Very few people know who Batman really is. His enemies include the Joker, the Penguin, Catwoman and Two-Face.

H 🎧 25 **Listen and complete the paragraph.**

Batman first appeared in comic books in (1)_____. He trains very hard and learns to use his (2)_____. He wears a costume that is (3)_____ to scare people. He drives a special (4)_____ called the Batmobile. His friend Robin was an acrobat in a (5)_____. Batman's real (6)_____ is actually Bruce Wayne. Batman fights many (7)_____ characters, but he always (8)_____ in the end.

I **Work with a classmate. Combine details that are similar from Activities G and H above.**

Batman is one of the world's first superheroes.

That's right. He first appeared in comic books in 1939.

Movie Guides

Unit 10

A What is playing at the movie theater this week? Discuss your answers.

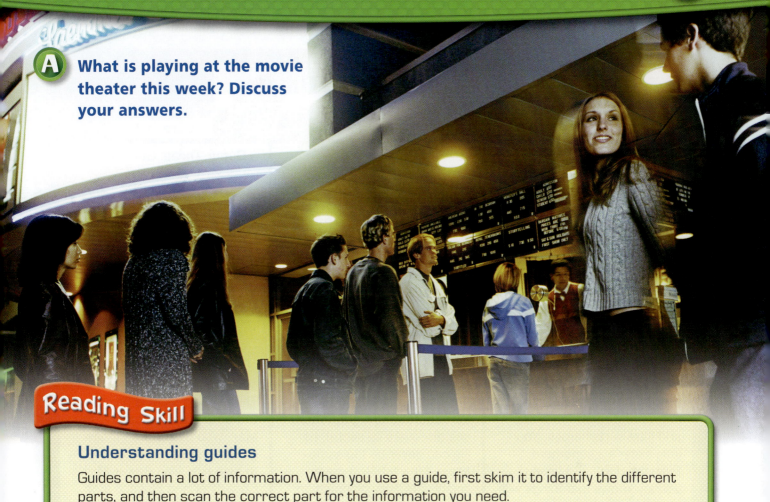

Reading Skill

Understanding guides

Guides contain a lot of information. When you use a guide, first skim it to identify the different parts, and then scan the correct part for the information you need.

B Label the parts of the movie guide.

- **A** how old you must be to watch the movie
- **B** information about prices
- **C** information about the story
- **D** where you can watch the movie
- **E** what times the movie will be shown
- **F** scene from the movie

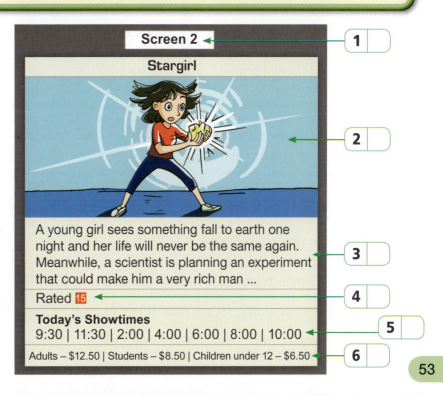

Reading

C 🎧 26 **Read the movie guide.**

Silver Star Movie Theater

Screen 1
Johnny the Superhero

Mrs. Blaze looks at her son angrily and says, "Your dad and I are superheroes. Your little sister's a superhero. Even the dog!" But young Johnny knows that things will be different when he goes to Super School. Or will they?

Rated **12**

Today's Showtimes
11:20 | 1:30 | 3:40 | 5:50 | 8:05 | 10:20

Screen 2
Stargirl

A young girl sees something fall to earth one night. When she discovers its secret, her life can never be the same again. Meanwhile, a crazy scientist is busy planning an experiment that could make him a very, very rich man ...

Rated **15**

Today's Showtimes
11:30 | 1:20 | 3:10 | 5:00 | 6:50 | 8:40 | 10:30

Screen 3
Super Three: Game Over

The exciting team is back! But so is the evil Doctor Max, who has formed a new group of powerful creatures to help him. Can Power-Man, Speedster and Elastico stop him this time?

Rated **15**

Today's Showtimes
11:00 | 2:30 | 4:30 | 6:30 | 8:30 | 10:30

Adults – $12.50 | Students & Seniors – $8.50 | Children under 12 – $6.50
Don't forget HALF-PRICE MONDAYS and TWO-FOR-ONE TUESDAYS!

G General – Suitable for all audiences
PG Parental Guidance – Audiences under 12 must be with a parent
12 Audiences must be 12 or over
15 Audiences must be 15 or over
R Restricted – Audiences must be 18 or over

D **Answer the questions.**

1. Which movie is about a family of superheroes?
2. Which movie has a secret that is discovered?
3. Who is the Super Three's main enemy?

Practice

E Write the answers.

1. Which movie is showing on Screen 2? _____
2. How many shows are there for *Johnny the Superhero*? _____
3. How many morning shows are there for *Stargirl*? _____
4. Which movie can you see at 8:30 p.m.? _____
5. Which movie has the most shows? _____
6. Which movies can you watch if you are 15 years old? _____
7. How much does it cost for an adult to watch a movie on Monday? _____
8. How much does it cost in total for four students to watch a movie together on Tuesday? _____

TIP Note what kind of information you need, then skim and scan the movie guide.

F Find and write the word next to its definition.

1. _____ *n*   someone who is old and does not work anymore
2. _____ *n*   help or advice that is given to someone
3. _____ *n*   a large white surface that pictures are shown on
4. _____ *n*   a place where you go to watch movies
5. _____ *adj* having the right qualities for a particular person, purpose or situation
6. _____ *adj* not limited to one use, activity or subject
7. _____ *adj* limited or controlled by rules
8. _____ *v*   to judge what age group a movie is suitable for

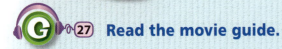

G 🎧 27 Read the movie guide.

Screen 2

Electro Boy and Mechano Girl

A student creates a robot for a competition. However, an evil scientist steals the robot and turns it into a dangerous fighting machine. Electro Boy and Mechano Girl must find a way to work together if they are to stop it from destroying the city.

Rated 15

10:00 | 12:30 | 3:00 | 5:30 | 8:00 | 10:30

Adults – $12.00 | Students & Seniors – $8.00 | Children under 12 – $6.00
All morning shows HALF PRICE!

H Make a guide for your favorite movie.

Theater	
Screen	
Movie	
Story	
Rating	
Showtimes	
Price	

I Present your movie guide to the class.

Review 5

 Read the movie guides.

MovieMax Theater:
Super Three: Game Over

Can Power-Man, Speedster and Elastico save the world yet again? Find out in this latest Super Three adventure. The team's amazing abilities have been given a boost! Power-Man is stronger, Speedster is faster and Elastico can now stretch even further. So will it really be game over for the evil Doctor M this time?

Rated 15

Showtimes: 9:00 | 10:30 | 12:30 | 2:00 | 3:30 | 5:00 | 7:00 | 9:00
Tickets: Adults – $11.00, Students – $9.00, Children under 16 – $5.50
Don't forget Terrific Tuesdays—buy one ticket and get a free box of popcorn!

Stargirl
Now Showing at Mega-Theater!

After finding a mysterious rock, Lucy Berry's life changes forever. During the day, Lucy is a normal 16-year-old. However, on starry nights she becomes the powerful Stargirl. She flies at the speed of light and can see through walls. See how she uses her new abilities to fight the crazy scientist, Doctor Cash.

Rated 15

Showtimes: 10:30 | 12:30 | 2:30 | 4:30 | 6:30 | 8:30 | 10:30
Tickets: Adults – $10.00, Students – $8.00
Half price all day Mondays!

B Circle the correct answer.

1. From the *Super Three: Game Over* guide, we can infer that
   a. the evil Doctor M has superhero abilities, too.
   b. there have been other Super Three movies.
   c. Power-Man is the leader of the team.
   d. the Super Three are all the same age.

2. From the *Stargirl* guide, we can infer that
   a. Stargirl defeats Doctor Cash.
   b. Lucy likes her new superhero abilities.
   c. the mysterious rock helps Lucy become Stargirl.
   d. Stargirl used to be in the Super Three.

3. From previous knowledge about *Super Three: Game Over*, we know that
   a. the Super Three save the world.
   b. the evil doctor's name is Max.
   c. this is the last Super Three movie.
   d. Speedster and Elastico are married.

4. From previous knowledge about *Stargirl*, we know that
   a. Lucy goes to school during the day.
   b. Doctor Cash is a scientist.
   c. Lucy knew Doctor Cash before.
   d. the mysterious rock fell from the sky.

C Write the answers.

1. How much does it cost a 15-year-old to watch *Super Three: Game Over* on Thursday?
   _____

2. How much does it cost a student to watch *Stargirl* on Monday? _____

3. At which theater can you get two tickets for the normal price of one?
   _____

Blogging — Unit 11

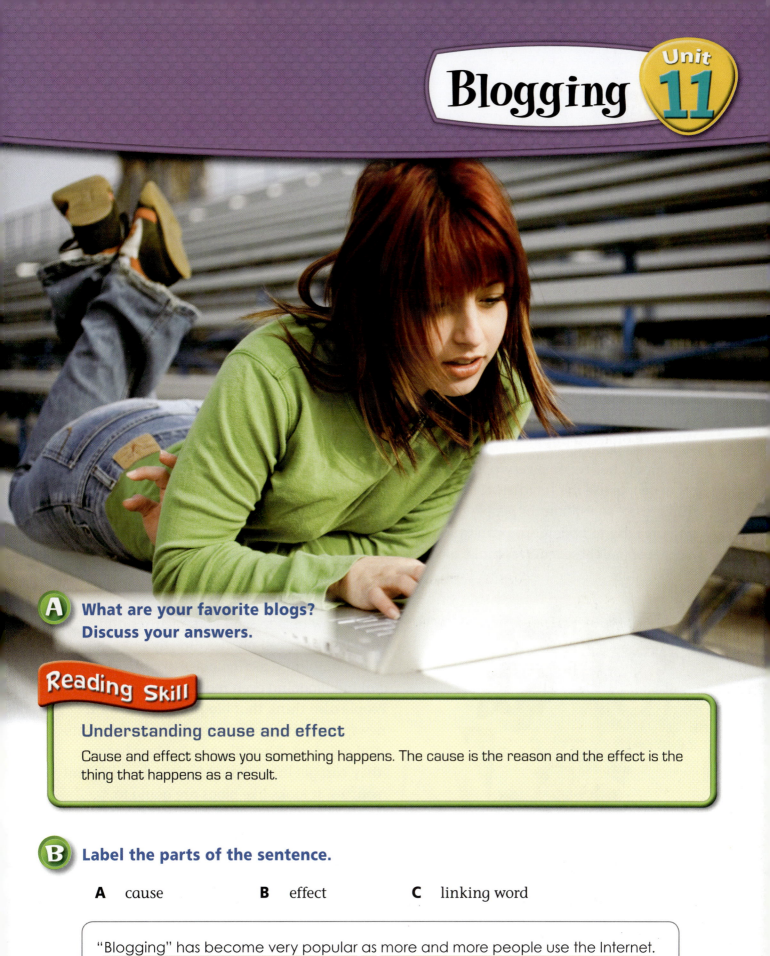

A What are your favorite blogs? Discuss your answers.

Reading Skill

Understanding cause and effect

Cause and effect shows you something happens. The cause is the reason and the effect is the thing that happens as a result.

B Label the parts of the sentence.

A cause   B effect   C linking word

"Blogging" has become very popular as more and more people use the Internet.

1   2   3

 Read the passage.

The Rise of the Blog

What is a blog?

A "blog" is a shortened name for a "web log." They are a kind of personal online diary. People write blogs about all kinds of things, from news and events to hobbies and reviews. Some people use them just as a simple record of what they have done.

Why are blogs so popular?

"Blogging" has become very popular as more and more people use the Internet. New technology has made keeping a blog an easy thing to do, so millions of people now have their own blogs. They are usually free to set up and are easy to update. You can upload pictures onto a blog and link to other websites. To many people, these features make blogs much more useful than traditional diaries.

How are blogs developing?

We are now able to send text, pictures and video from our cell phones directly onto the Web. Combining technologies like this is making blogging even more convenient. People also think that blogs are better than newspapers for finding out about news, events and opinions. They like to use blogs because they can get information from many different sources. It looks like blogs are going to become one of the most important ways to find and share information in the future.

D **Answer the questions.**

1. What is a blog?
2. What has made blogging an easy thing to do?
3. What can we send onto the Web from cell phones?

Practice

E **Complete the cause and effect table.**

	Cause		Effect
1	New technology has made keeping a blog a fun thing to do.	→	Millions of people now have their own blogs.
2	You can upload pictures onto a blog and link to other websites.	→	
3	Cell phone and web technologies are being combined.	→	
4		→	People like to use blogs.

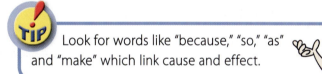

TIP: Look for words like "because," "so," "as" and "make" which link cause and effect.

F **Find and write the word next to its definition.**

1 _____ n scientific ideas used in practical ways

2 _____ n where something comes from

3 _____ n information that is written down and stored for the future

4 _____ adj about one particular person

5 _____ v to move information onto a computer network for others to see

6 _____ v to add the most recent information to something

7 _____ v to connect two or more things

8 _____ adv without going through other processes

61

 G 30 Read about the blogs Kate and Ben would like to start.

I'd like to start a blog about my favorite hobby, horse-riding. With this blog, I could share information with other people who like horses. Maybe I could get some riding tips, too.

I'd like to start a blog about great soccer stars! With this blog, I could share information with other people who like soccer. Maybe I could find out about new players, too.

 H What kind of blog would you like to start? What information could you share or learn? Write what you and three classmates think.

Name	Kind of blog	Information I could share	Information I could learn
1 Me			
2			
3			
4			

 I Tell the class.

> Jack would like to start a blog about his favorite superhero, Batman. He could share information with other people who like Batman movies. Maybe he could find out about new Batman comic books, too.

Online Forums

Unit 12

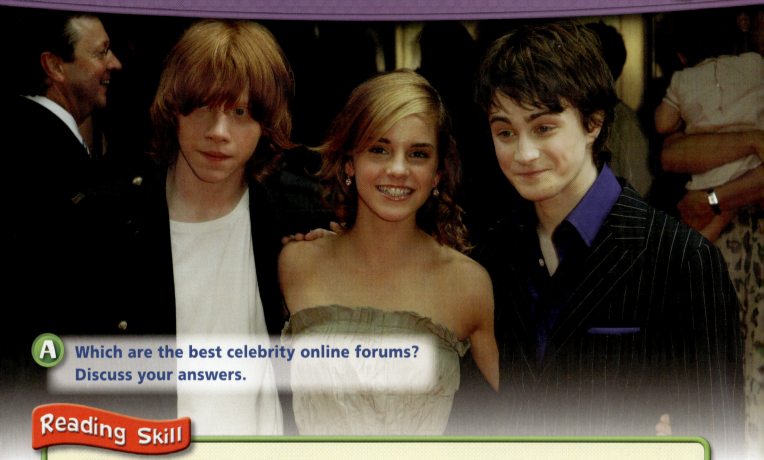

A Which are the best celebrity online forums? Discuss your answers.

Reading Skill

Understanding online forums
An online forum is a place on the Internet where people can share information or opinions about something.

B Label the parts of the online forum.

A what the message is about
B how many replies there are
C who wrote the first message
D who wrote the latest reply
E when was the latest reply
F number of pages

Topic		Replies	Author	Last Post
The Dragon School	1 2	11	James	June 12, 1:43 p.m. by Mike
Emma is Hermione	1 2 3 4 5 6	58	Ben	June 12, 10:29 a.m. by Ben

1 → The Dragon School
2 → 1 2 3 4 5 6
3 → 58
4 → Ben
5 → by Ben
6 → June 12, 1:43 p.m.

Reading

 31 Look at the online forum and read the messages.

	Topic		Replies	Author	Last Post
★	The Dragon School	1 2	11	James	June 12, 1:43 p.m. by Mike
✌	Emma is Hermione	1 2 3 4 5 6	58	Ben	June 12, 10:29 a.m. by Ben
☺	I met Emma! Really!	1 2 3 4 5 6 7 8 9	83	Amy	June 11, 9:41 p.m. by Amy
✺	Emma is a sports star	1 2 3	22	Sarah	June 11, 9:11 p.m. by Kate

A

Emma is Hermione

Emma is great as Hermione, don't you think? She plays the role perfectly.

As I said in my previous post, I still think Emma is perfect for the role. Now when I read my Harry Potter books, I always see her as Hermione!

Reply

B

I read that Emma is actually quite good at sports. Does anyone know which sports?

I saw in a magazine that she's really good at field hockey (my favorite sport). I also heard she's good at tennis.

Reply

C

I heard a lot of important people went to this school when they were young. It's in England, isn't it? So why the name "dragon"? Sounds kind of scary!

This is an interesting thread. Maybe the school is a bit like Hogwarts …

Reply

D

She's actually quite normal in real life. When she spoke to me, I thought she was friendly and funny. Has anyone here met her, too?

Wow! You're so lucky! Where did you meet her? Tell us more!

Reply

D Write the topics for the messages above.

Practice

E Complete the sentences.

1. To start a new thread in the forum, click "_____."
2. To write a reply to a message, click "_____."
3. To find a topic in the forum, click "_____."
4. _____ started the thread about Emma being a sports star.
5. There are _____ replies about the Dragon School.
6. There are _____ pages in the thread about Emma being Hermione.
7. _____ is the eleventh person to write about the Dragon School.
8. The "_____" thread is the most popular.

TIP Look carefully at the column headings and the links to find the information.

F Find and write the word next to its definition.

1	_____	n	someone who writes a book, an article, a message, etc.
2	_____	n	a message sent to an Internet discussion group to be read by others
3	_____	n	the possible choices you can make
4	_____	n	information sent to another person
5	_____	n	a group of messages about the same subject
6	_____	adj	the one that came right before
7	_____	v	to try to find information
8	_____	v	to exit from an online computer program

G Think of a famous person you would like to start an online forum about. Name the forum and write three topic ideas.

The _____ Forum

	Topic
☺	
☺	
☺	

H Choose one of your topics above and write the message for it. Then ask four classmates to reply to your message.

Author: Date/Time:	
	Reply
Posted by: Date/Time:	
	Reply
Posted by: Date/Time:	
	Reply
Posted by: Date/Time:	
	Reply
Posted by: Date/Time:	
	Reply

Review 6

A **Read the webpage.**

http://www.myeasyspace.com/people/teens/qoc.htm

People > Teenagers > Queen of Chocolate

Chocolate Talk!

Welcome to my chocolate blog and forum! I started my blog because I wanted to share my love of chocolate with you all! I also started the forum so chocolate lovers can get together, ask questions and share their knowledge about chocolate. So please leave a message and join in with the chocolate talk!

Christina

The Choco Forum

Topic	Replies	Author
All about chocolate! 1 2 3 4 5 6 7 8 9 10	95	Christina
The very best? 1 2 3 4 5 6 7 8 9 10 11 12	117	Mia
Chocolate brands 1 2 3 4 5 6 7	64	Andy
White or dark? 1 2 3 4 5 6 7 8 9 10 11	99	Christina
Cool chocolate wrappers! 1 2 3	11	Grace

The QOC Blog

Sat., Sept. 16

Found a new chocolate in the store today—it's called Crunchit. I tried it when I got home. It's pretty good, but a little too crunchy!

Tues., Sept. 5

You know that I'm not a big fan of white chocolate most of the time, but there's a new brand out called Sky Bar. I tried it because I liked the wrapper—it's so cute!

B **Circle the correct answer. You can circle more than one.**

From the webpage, we can infer that Christina

a is the biggest chocolate fan in the world.
b likes using computers and the Internet.
c likes all kinds of chocolate.
d likes talking to other people about chocolate.

C **Complete the cause and effect table.**

	Cause		Effect
1	Christina wanted to share her love of chocolate with us all.	→	
2		→	Chocolate lovers can get together, ask questions and share their knowledge about chocolate.
3		→	Christina tried a Sky Bar.

D **Write the answers.**

1 Which topic is the most popular in The Choco Forum?

_____

2 Which topic does this message belong to?

Did you know that chocolate comes from the tropical cacao tree?   _____

Mini-dictionary

A
ability	n	a skill or power to do something	p. 50
adventure	n	an exciting experience	p. 50
amuse	v	to make someone laugh or smile	p. 10
ancient	adj	happening or existing a long time ago	p. 40
army	n	a large group of soldiers who are trained to fight on land	p. 40
author	n	someone who writes a book, an article, a message, etc.	p. 64

B
balance	v	to be in a position where you will not fall over	p. 14
brave	adj	showing no fear in a dangerous situation	p. 10
burn	v	to destroy something with fire	p. 20

C
capital	n	a city where the main government of a country is	p. 30
caption	n	an explanation for a picture	p. 50
carpool	v	to travel together in one car and share the cost	p. 24
celebrate	v	to show that something is important by doing something special	p. 10
coast	n	land next to the sea	p. 30
collect	v	to get things and bring them together	p. 44
combine	v	to mix things together	p. 10
complicated	adj	difficult to understand because it has many details	p. 34
concentrate	v	to use most of your attention and time to do one thing	p. 14
control	v	to make someone or something do what you want	p. 50
convenient	adj	near and easy to get to	p. 34
costume	n	clothes that make you look like someone else	p. 10

D
directly	adv	without going through other processes	p. 60
downside	n	the negative or bad part of something	p. 14
dream	n	a wish to do, be or have something	p. 10

E
electricity	n	the power that is used to make machines work or to provide light or heat	p. 24
enemy	n	someone who wants to harm you	p. 50
environment	n	the air, water and land on earth	p. 24

F

flood	v	to become covered in water	p. 20
found	v	to start something such as a city or company	p. 30

G

gadget	n	a cleverly designed machine or tool	p. 50
general	adj	not limited to one use, activity or subject	p. 54
global	adj	about the whole world	p. 20
goal	n	something you hope to complete successfully in the future	p. 24
guidance	n	help or advice that is given to someone	p. 54

H

hard-working	adj	working with a lot of effort	p. 44
head	v	to go towards a particular place	p. 34
heat	n	high temperature	p. 20
homesick	adj	feeling unhappy because you are far from home	p. 14

I

idle	adj	lazy or not working	p. 44
influence	v	to affect the way someone thinks or acts	p. 40
interview	v	to ask someone questions for a newspaper	p. 14

L

landmark	n	something that helps you recognize where you are	p. 30
level	n	the amount of something compared to another amount	p. 20
lie	n	something you say that you know is untrue	p. 44
link	v	to connect two or more things	p. 60
literature	n	books, poems and plays that are important	p. 40
log out	phr v	to exit from an online computer program	p. 64

M

melt	v	to change into liquid form	p. 20
memorize	v	to learn something completely so that you remember it exactly	p. 40
message	n	information sent to another person	p. 64
military	adj	about a country's army or navy	p. 40
miss	v	to not notice a train or bus stop until it has passed	p. 34
movement	n	when something moves from one place to another	p. 14
movie theater	n	a place where you go to watch movies	p. 54
mutant	n	an animal or person whose body is different from others of the same kind	p. 50

O

options	n	the possible choices you can make	p. 64

P

passenger	n	someone who is traveling in a vehicle, but not driving	p. 34
performance	n	a show of acting, dancing or singing	p. 10
personal	adj	about one particular person	p. 60
philosophy	n	the study of ideas about thought and actions	p. 40
plastic	adj	made from a light strong material	p. 24
platform	n	the raised place where you get on and off a train	p. 34
population	n	number of people living in an area	p. 30
port	n	an area or town where ships arrive and leave	p. 30
post	n	a message sent to an Internet discussion group to be read by others	p. 64
prepare	v	to make plans for something	p. 44
previous	adj	the one that came right before	p. 64

R

rate	v	to judge what age group a movie is suitable for	p. 54
record	n	information that is written down and stored for the future	p. 60
recycle	v	to treat something that has been used so it can be used again	p. 24
reduce	v	to make less or smaller in size	p. 24
reporter	n	someone who writes for a newspaper	p. 14
restricted	adj	limited or controlled by rules	p. 54
route	n	the way from one place to another	p. 34

S

screen	n	a large white surface that pictures are shown on	p. 54
search	v	to try to find information	p. 64
senior	n	someone who is old and does not work anymore	p. 54
shepherd	n	someone who takes care of sheep	p. 44
skyline	n	the outline of buildings against the sky	p. 30
source	n	where something comes from	p. 60
space	n	the place beyond the earth	p. 20
spectacular	adj	very impressive and dramatic	p. 30
stop	n	a place where a train or bus picks up or drops off people	p. 34
suitable	adj	having the right qualities for a particular person, purpose or situation	p. 54
superhero	n	a character in storybooks who uses special powers to help others	p. 50

T

technology	n	scientific ideas used in practical ways	p. 60
thread	n	a group of messages about the same subject	p. 64
tough	adj	difficult to do	p. 14
traditional	adj	following old methods or ideas	p. 10
trap	v	to keep something from getting out	p. 20
trash	n	things you throw away	p. 24
trick	n	something you do to make someone believe something that is not true	p. 44
trust	v	to believe that someone will not do anything bad	p. 44

U

update	v	to add the most recent information to something	p. 60
upload	v	to move information onto a computer network for others to see	p. 60

W

wrestle	v	to fight by holding or pushing	p. 40